PREDATOR VS PREY

HOW EAGLES AND OTHER BIRDS ATTACK

TIM HARRIS

PowerKiDS press

Published in 2026
by The Rosen Publishing Group, Inc.
2544 Clinton Street, Buffalo, NY 14224

First published in Great Britain in 2021 by Wayland

Editor: Amy Pimperton
Design: www.smartdesignstudio.co.uk
Picture research: Diana Morris

Cataloging-in-Publication Data

Names: Harris, Tim.

Title: How eagles and other birds attack / Tim Harris.

Description: Buffalo, NY : PowerKids Press, 2026. | Series: Predator vs. prey | Includes glossary and index.

Identifiers: ISBN 9781499454215 (pbk.) | ISBN 9781499454222 (library bound) | ISBN 9781499454239 (ebook)

Subjects: LCSH: Birds of prey--Juvenile literature.

Classification: LCC QL677.78 H377 2026 | DDC 598.9--dc23

Picture credits:
Alamy: Dave Watts 14. Dreamstime: Jay Pierstorff 5bl, 24; Sergey Uryadnikov 22. FLPA Images: Des Ong 7t; Paul Sawer 16. iStock: Dansin 11t; Ell77 1cr, 18; KatPaws 6. Nature PL: Stephen Dalton 1cl, 20; Guy Edwardes 4t; Wilm van den Heever 10; Nick Upton 13t; Konrad Wothe 12. Shutterstock: Alfmaler 19c; A7880S 7cr, 11c, 15t; 25cr; Artur Balytskyi 21cr; Baurz1973 27cl; Mark Cane 5c; Paul Cowell 11b; Ingrid Curry 25tl; Derriva 11cl; Le Do 17t; Franco Fratini 23t; Jay Gao back cover tr, 5br; Giedrilus 7b; grahamspics 15cr; Hennadii H 17cl; 25cl; HappyPictures 15cl, 27cr; Miroslav Hlavko 17br;Eric Isselee 8, 30; Aleksey Karpenko 21t; Ketta 27t; Weerachai Khanfu 11cr; Arild Lilleboe 23br; Aitor Lamadrid Lopez 1c, 26, 27b; Lynx Vector 23cr, 23b; MartelloStudio front cover c; Martin Mecnarowski back cover tc, 29b; Scott Mirror 13b; Nadya Art 9cl, 13cl, 29cl, 29cr; Michal Ninger 5t, 28; Stu Porter 29t; Ondrej Prosicky back cover tl, 9b, 21b, 25b; Daria Riabets 7cl; M Rose 15b; Rvector 19bl; Petr Salinger front cover tl; Mary San 9cr; Sasimoto 13cr; Nadzeya Shanchuk 17bl; Angel Simon 19t; Donovan van Staden 4b; Sumikophoto front cover tr; Park Ji Sun 21cl; Tobyphotos 19br; Rudmer Zwerver 9t.

Manufactured in the United States of America

CPSIA Compliance Information: Batch #CSPK26. For further information contact Rosen Publishing at 1-800-237-9932.

CONTENTS

BIRD PREDATORS

Birds are a type of animal. They are warm-blooded, plus have feathers and a beak. Females lay eggs from which baby birds hatch. All birds have wings and most, but not all, can fly. There are around 10,000 different species of birds on Earth. Many are herbivores that eat plants or seeds. Other birds are carnivores that eat meat. Carnivores must hunt and kill prey animals to survive.

Predatory birds live in all kinds of habitats. Some hunt in mountains and other remote places, others hunt over the oceans or even in the middle of cities. They come in many sizes, from giant eagles to small thrushes.

Most birds of prey, such as barn owls, are large and powerful, with excellent vision and hearing. Smaller birds, such as bee-eaters, hunt invertebrates. They are agile enough to catch fast-flying prey.

BARN OWL

A CARMINE BEE-EATER CAPTURES A FAST-FLYING INSECT

GOLDEN EAGLE

Some birds, such as golden eagles, are apex predators. This means that no other animals hunt them (apart from humans). Other predators, such as the American robin, eat invertebrates, but are themselves hunted by hawks. This is known as a food chain.

GANNET

AMERICAN ROBIN

HARRIS'S HAWK

This book explores the incredible ways birds have evolved to survive. Some use stealth, others use teamwork, some have special adaptations, such as the ability to fly silently, and others may dive at incredible speeds. Read on to find out how predatory birds overpower their prey.

GOLDEN EAGLE vs. RED GROUSE: TALONS

Power, speed, size, and aggression. The golden eagle has them all. From wing tip to wing tip, this massive bird of prey is more than 6 feet (1.8 m) across. Its sharp, hooked beak is about 2 inches (5 cm) long. The four talons on each foot can squeeze much harder than a human hand can.

FEAR FROM ABOVE

This eagle is named for the gold-colored feathers that fleck its brown plumage. It lives in remote mountain ranges and deserts, where pairs defend and hunt over huge territories. These birds can be found across North America, Europe, and parts of Asia and Africa.

The silhouette of a golden eagle soaring high in the sky is enough to strike fear into any animal below. Golden eagles sometimes attack adult deer and have been known to push ibex off mountain ledges. Usually, though, they hunt smaller animals, such as hares and grouse.

RED GROUSE

Red grouse are plump birds that live on high moorland in the United Kingdom, where they feed on shoots of heather. Golden eagles often target them, but if the grouse see an attack coming they stand a good chance of escaping. This is because they can fly very fast and close to the ground, with their wings making a whirring noise. Although eagles are quick when they dive, they can't outpace a flying grouse.

RAPTOR: A BIRD OF PREY

GOLDEN EAGLE STATS

Length: 3 ft (1 m)
Wingspan: 6 - 7.5 ft (1.8 - 2.3 m)
Weight: 11 lbs (5 kg) (females are heavier)
Top speed: 149 mph (240 kph) when diving

Superb eyesight; dives at speed; powerful legs; sharp talons; strong beak

VS.

RED GROUSE STATS

Length: 15 in (38 cm)
Wingspan: 24 in (61 cm)
Weight: 1.3 lb (0.6 kg)
Top speed: 68 mph (109 kph)

Camouflaged on ground; flies low and fast, making capture difficult

NO ESCAPE

Plunging down at breakneck speed, an eagle tries to grasp its prey before it can escape. Once caught in the raptor's strong, sharp talons, a grouse, hare, or even a fox has no chance of escaping. In the breeding season, the eagle will fly back to its nest with the meal. At other times, it will eat where it has made the kill.

BARN OWL VS. WOOD MOUSE: HEARING

In the half-light of dusk, the fluttering flight of a hunting barn owl looks ghostly. These birds are almost white underneath and a pale sandy color above. Their hearing is so sensitive that they can hear the sound of a mouse moving through grass. They also have excellent night vision.

SOUND AND VISION

A barn owl has a flat face, with both eyes facing forward. This arrangement gives the bird binocular vision, helping it to judge the distance of its prey – very important for a hunter. The owl's ears are hidden beneath a covering of feathers. Each ear is a slightly different shape and one ear is higher than the other. This helps the owl to pinpoint exactly where its prey is – even in total darkness.

BARN OWLS ARE FOUND ON ALL CONTINENTS, EXCEPT ANTARCTICA.

HEARING: THE ABILITY TO DETECT SOUNDS

LARGE EARS CAN DETECT INCREDIBLY QUIET SOUNDS

CAN SHED THE SKIN ON ITS TAIL TO HELP ESCAPE FROM A PREDATOR THAT GRABS IT BY THE TAIL

WOOD MOUSE

Although wood mice have no means of defending themselves, they have relatively large ears and a very good sense of hearing. If a predator makes any sound at all, the mouse will hear it. And they are good at running from danger. Their legs can carry them quickly to the safety of their burrow. But it may not get the chance to escape if the attacker is a silent barn owl.

PINPOINT: TO IDENTIFY SOMETHING ACCURATELY

BARN OWL STATS

Length: 14 in (36 cm)
Wingspan: 3.6 ft (1.1 m)
Weight: 0.8 lbs (360 g)
Top speed: 22 mph (35.4 kph)

Flies silently; great night vision; long legs and strong talons for grasping prey

VS.

WOOD MOUSE STATS

Length: 4 in (10 cm)
Weight: 0.04 lbs (20 g)
Top speed: 3 mph (5 kph)

Good hearing; can escape quickly into vegetation

HOVER AND STRIKE

An owl's wings make no noise as it flies. So, while it can hear its prey – a rat, mouse, vole, or shrew – the prey can't hear it. The owl hovers silently over the place it has heard a sound, then drops to the ground to grab the victim with its taloned feet.

GANNET VS. SQUID: HIGH DIVING

A fishing gannet looks like a huge white dart shooting into the ocean. It hits the water with a splash of spray, then emerges a few seconds later with a fish or squid. By high-diving from 100 feet (30 m), it reaches a speed of 60 mph (97 kph) as it hits the water – fast enough to take it down to the fish or squid swimming far below. Its long, strong beak is like a dagger, with sharp cutting edges – ideal for seizing prey and slicing it up.

STREAMLINED BODY

If a person dived into water from that height, they would probably hurt themselves badly. A diving gannet is unharmed because it folds its wings back and has a streamlined body that cuts through the water with little impact. It also has waterproof feathers and can close its nostrils so water doesn't get in!

STREAMLINED: SOMETHING THAT MOVES EASILY THROUGH WATER OR AIR

CAPE GANNETS (ABOVE) LIVE ALONG THE COASTS OF SOUTHERN AFRICA. NORTHERN GANNETS INHABIT COASTS OF THE NORTH ATLANTIC, AND AUSTRALASIAN GANNETS ARE FOUND OFF THE WESTERN, SOUTHERN, AND EASTERN COASTS OF AUSTRALIA.

SQUID

Squid are sea creatures with an amazing method for escaping predators. When attacked, they release black ink that clouds the water and hides them. The predator is left confused as the squid swims to safety. Unfortunately for them, if a diving gannet targets them, they have no time to play the ink trick and are likely to end up in the bird's beak.

GANNET STATS

Length: 3 ft (1 m)
Wingspan: 6 ft (1.8 m)
Weight: 8 lbs (3.6 kg)
Top speed: 62 mph (100 kph) when diving

Excellent eyesight; air sacs under the skin help to cushion the impact with the water

VS.

SHORTFIN SQUID STATS

Length: 12 in (30 cm)
Weight: 0.8 lb (350 g)
Top speed: 2.5 mph (4 kph)

Excellent vision; aggressive; squirts ink to confuse predatory fish, but gannet attacks are often too fast

JOINING IN

When a gannet discovers a shoal of herring, cod, or pollack, it will dive to catch one. Any other gannets nearby will see this and fly closer to investigate. If the shoal is large, 20 or 30 birds may attack, which must be both terrifying and confusing to the prey.

PEREGRINE FALCON VS. TEAL: SPEED

Almost any bird is a target for a hunting peregrine falcon. Found all around the world, this bird of prey is the fastest animal on Earth. It is capable of reaching 224 mph (360 kph) as it dives, or stoops, on prey. That's faster than a Formula 1 racing car.

STOOP AND STUN

Peregrines live in mountains, on coastal cliffs, and on tall buildings in cities – all places where they can build their nests on ledges. When they notice prey, they take off from the ledge, climb high into the air, and then go into a steep dive with their wings folded close to their body so they are streamlined. By the time they strike their target – a duck, pigeon, or other bird – they are going so fast that the impact stuns or kills the prey. The peregrine then flies back to its ledge, holding the kill securely in its talons.

STOOP: WHEN A BIRD SWOOPS DOWN ON ITS PREY

IN NORTH AMERICA, THE PEREGRINE IS ALSO KNOWN AS THE DUCK HAWK.

SPEED: THE RATE AT WHICH SOMETHING MOVES

TEAL

Teal are ducks that live on lakes and ponds, and in coastal marshes and estuaries. They often join together in flocks to feed on seeds that they find on the water's surface. Teal are nervous birds. If they are alarmed, they will take to the air. They usually fly fast – often twisting and turning – with very rapid wingbeats. This is when a peregrine is likely to attack.

PEREGRINE STATS

Length: 18 in (46 cm) (females are longer)
Weight: 3 lbs (1.4 kg) (females are heavier)
Top speed: 224 mph (360 kph)

Excellent eyesight; dives at breakneck speed; sharp talons and hooked beak for tearing flesh

VS.

TEAL STATS

Length: 16 in (40.6 cm)
Weight: 0.7 lbs (350 g)
Top speed: 50 mph (80 kph)

Alert to danger; often flies in flocks, confusing predators; fast flight, twisting and turning to escape aerial attack

STARTLED TEAL TAKE OFF AS A FLOCK. SAFETY IN NUMBERS REDUCES THE RISK OF AN INDIVIDUAL BEING ATTACKED.

SONG THRUSH VS. SNAIL: TOOLS

Best known for their speckled plumage and the loudly repeated phrases of their song, thrushes are birds of woodlands and gardens. They eat a variety of food, including berries, fruit, earthworms, caterpillars, and snails. Mostly, they simply grab food with their beak and swallow it whole. The problem with snails, though, is that the soft body parts are protected by a hard outer shell.

SHELL-CRACKER

The thrush has an ingenious answer to this problem. It grabs the snail and bangs it hard against a favorite stone (called an anvil) until the shell cracks open. The bird then eats the flesh inside.

ANVIL: A HEAVY IRON BLOCK THAT METAL IS HAMMERED AND SHAPED ON

INTELLIGENT

WILL EAT A RANGE OF OTHER INVERTEBRATES, SUCH AS WORMS AND CATERPILLARS

THRUSHES LIVE ACROSS EURASIA AND NORTHERN AFRICA. THEY WERE INTRODUCED INTO NEW ZEALAND, BUT ARE NOT NATIVE BIRDS TO THE ISLANDS.

TOOL: AN OBJECT USED TO DO A PARTICULAR JOB

GARDEN SNAIL

Snails have a soft body with two eyes on the end of stalks. They glide over the ground on a slimy "foot" as they go in search of leaves to eat. When a snail is threatened, it pulls its head inside its shell and seals up the entrance with lots of slimy mucus. Many predators will give up then and look elsewhere for a meal, but not the song thrush!

SONG THRUSH STATS

Length: 9 in (23 cm)
Weight: 3 oz (85 g)
Top speed: 40 kph

Strong beak; uses tools to break tough shells

VS.

GARDEN SNAIL STATS

Length: 1 in (2.5 cm)
Weight: 0.7 oz (20 g)
Top speed: 16 ft (5 m) per hour

Tough shell protects body parts; foul-tasting mucus

INSTINCT

In experiments, scientists gave some baby thrushes, just a few days old, snail-shaped stones. The baby birds smashed them on the ground even though they had never seen their parents doing this with real snails. This is called instinctive behavior.

HOBBY VS. DRAGONFLY: AGILITY

With long, pointed wings, which are swept back as it flies, the hobby is one of the top predators of the air. It is not a powerful bird of prey, but what it lacks in bulk and strength it more than makes up for in agility. It is an amazing flier, capable of rapid acceleration and high-speed aerial maneuvers as it chases dragonflies, swallows, and martins.

RELIANCE ON SPEED

A hobby can out-fly even the fastest target. When it catches up with it, the predator's talons grab the prey and pass it to its beak. Hobbies often eat on the wing – and they fly a lot!

MIGRATION

Hobbies spend the winter months in Africa and migrate thousands of miles to Europe and northern Asia each spring to raise a family. Then they return to Africa in the autumn with their offspring. Along the route there are always plenty of flying insects and birds for them to hunt.

AGILE: ABLE TO MOVE QUICKLY AND EASILY

DRAGONFLY

Dragonflies are brightly colored, fast-flying insects that are often seen as a bright flash of color as they whiz past on a summer's day. Some have "warning" colors of red or yellow to fool birds into thinking they are toxic. Their nimble flying skills make them difficult to catch. Huge compound eyes make dragonflies excellent at spotting potential predators. Large "dragons" are themselves predators, expertly hunting midges and other small flies.

COMPOUND EYE: AN EYE MADE UP OF LOTS OF TINY LENSES

HOBBY STATS

Wingspan: 30 in (76 cm)
Length: 14 in (36 cm)
Weight: 9 oz (255 g)
Top speed: 87 mph (140 kph)

Fast flight, following twists and turns of prey; sharp eyesight; strong legs and feet

VS.

DRAGONFLY STATS

Wingspan: 4 in (10 cm)
Length: 3 in (8 cm)
Weight: a few ounces
Top speed: 25 mph (40 kph)

Excellent ability to detect movement; alert; fast flight; agile

HOBBIES – SUCH AS THIS EURASIAN HOBBY – ARE A TYPE OF FALCON.

SHORT-TOED EAGLE VS. LIZARD: HOVERING

When searching for food, some birds of prey survey the ground below them from a perch – the top of a high tree or building. Others fly very high and soar around like glider planes, with their wings held out. A very few birds can hover, remaining almost motionless above the same position on the ground. They do this by flapping their wings quite fast. Kestrels do this and so do short-toed eagles.

SOAR: TO FLY (HIGH) WITHOUT FLAPPING OF THE WINGS

HOVERING HUNTER

A short-toed eagle hovers when it is hunting for its favorite food – snakes and lizards. When it spots a movement below, it drops to the ground. As it comes down, it stretches out its legs, like a pilot lowering the undercarriage of a plane when it comes in to land. The eagle grabs its prey with the talons on its feet and flies to a nearby perch to eat it.

A VERY QUIET BIRD COMPARED TO OTHER RAPTORS, IT ONLY OCCASIONALLY LETS OUT A CRY

SHORT TALONS PERFECTLY ADAPTED TO GRAB SNAKES AND OTHER SMALL REPTILES

IN THE SPRING, THESE EAGLES MIGRATE FROM AFRICA TO CENTRAL AND SOUTHERN EUROPE.

HOVER: TO STAY IN ONE PLACE IN THE AIR

WILL BITE TO DETER PREDATORS

CLAWS HELP IT TO CLIMB ROCKS AND TREES TO ESCAPE PREDATORS

SHORT-TOED EAGLE STATS

Length: 3 - 6 ft (1-1.8 m) (males are longer)
Weight: 123 - 212 lbs (56 - 96 kg) (males are heavier)
Top speed: 65 kph

Good eyesight; the ability to hover; strong, sharp talons and hooked beak

VS.

OCELLATED LIZARD STATS

Length: 60 cm
Weight: 18 oz (510 g)
Top speed: 4 mph (6 kph) in short bursts

Very fast in short bursts, darting into bushes and holes; good hearing

OCELLATED LIZARD

While snakes make up most of the eagle's diet, ocellated lizards also feature on the menu. These lizards are predators themselves, eating beetles and other large insects, birds' eggs, and smaller lizards, frogs, and mammals. They live in dry, bushy areas in southern Europe. They have an acute sense of hearing and can run very fast when pouncing on prey or fleeing from danger. If threatened, they hide in thick vegetation or cracks between rocks or will race up a tree.

KESTRELS ARE ALSO EXPERTS AT HOVERING. THEY ARE ABLE TO KEEP THEIR HEADS COMPLETELY STILL TO FOCUS ON THEIR PREY AS THEIR WINGS BEAT FURIOUSLY.

SPARROWHAWK VS. CHAFFINCH: AMBUSH

Eurasian sparrowhawks are pursuit predators that hunt mostly other birds. They are fast fliers with phenomenal flight control. This is thanks to a long tail, which enables them to change direction in the blink of an eye. This makes them great at out-flying birds in woodland, but not so good in open country.

PURSUIT: THE ACTION OF CHASING SOMETHING

CAUSING PANIC

A sparrowhawk is happy to spend hours perching on the branch of a tree, simply watching and waiting. When a flock of small finches comes to feed on the ground, though, the hawk will explode into action, dropping from its perch and flying rapidly toward them. One finch may see the danger and call to sound the alarm. If this happens, the other birds panic and scatter into the air, but the hawk has already singled out its target.

SHORT, ROUNDED WINGS HELP WITH FAST CHANGES OF DIRECTION

COUNTERSHADING (A PALE BELLY AND DARKER UPPER BODY PARTS) HELP TO CAMOUFLAGE THIS BIRD WHILE HUNTING

RUDDER-LIKE TAIL HELPS THE BIRD TO TWIST AND TURN IN DENSE WOODLAND

CHAFFINCH

In spring and summer, chaffinches feed on caterpillars and other grubs living on leaves. Outside of the breeding season, they often gather in flocks to eat seeds that have fallen to the ground. Like most birds, they are very alert, but find it hard to out-fly a sparrowhawk attacking seemingly out of nowhere.

SPARROWHAWK STATS

Length: 13 - 16 in (33 - 41 cm) (females are longer)
Wingspan: up to 30 in (76 cm)
Weight: 5 - 12 oz (150 - 340 g) (females are heavier)
Top speed: 31 mph (50 kph)

Very sharp eyesight and hearing; flies silently, with superb maneuverability in flight

VS.

CHAFFINCH STATS

Length: 6 in (15 cm)
Wingspan: 11 in (28 cm)
Weight: 1 oz (28 g)
Top speed: 31 mph (50 kph)

Alert; good hearing and eyesight; can fly into dense, protective vegetation

SILENT AMBUSH

A sparrowhawk may fly silently along one side of a hedge, waiting to hear the calls of small birds on the other side. If the hawk hears them, it suddenly flips over the top of the hedge to ambush an unwitting victim. Most of the small birds will escape, but one may end up being plucked and then eaten.

SKUA VS. PUFFIN: DROWNING

Skuas are the pirates of the oceans. Looking like a cross between a gull and a bird of prey, they have the webbed feet of a gull and the hooked beak of a hawk. Much of the time a skua goes unnoticed as it swims on the waters of the North Atlantic Ocean. But when it sees another seabird that it thinks has a crop full of food, it springs into action.

CROP: A POUCH IN A BIRD'S THROAT FOR STORING FOOD

BULLIES OF THE AIR

Taking off from the water, the skua flies in pursuit of gulls and terns, following their every twist and turn. Eventually, the other bird will cough up its last meal to get rid of the skua, which gratefully catches the food in mid-air. A hungry skua is even more brutal with smaller seabirds. If the predator catches sight of a puffin, there is a life-or-death race over the water.

A VERY AGGRESSIVE BIRD, THE SKUA SHOWS LITTLE FEAR EVEN OF HUMANS AND WILL DIVE-BOMB OTHER BIRDS TO DRIVE THEM FROM THEIR FOOD.

ATLANTIC PUFFIN

Puffins are plump little birds with an amazing, rainbow-colored beak. In spring, when raising a single chick, parent birds fly to and fro between their burrow and the sea. There, they dive to catch sandeels to feed their young. Skuas will attack them when they are flying with their catch. Sometimes, the fast-flying puffin makes it back to land. Puffins can swim underwater and dive to depths of 200 feet (61 m), which is handy when trying to evade a skua. At other times, the skua catches it and drowns it in the water.

AMAZING BEAK TO HOLD MANY SANDEELS

SILENT AT SEA

VERY POOR AT LANDING – THEY TEND TO CRASH LAND

A GREAT SKUA WILL TAKE ON BIRDS AS LARGE AND POWERFUL AS GANNETS.

GREAT SKUA STATS

Length: 23 in (58 cm)
Wingspan: 55 in (140 cm)
Weight: 3 lb (1.4 kg)
Top speed: 37 mph (60 kph)

Aggressive; strong legs and talons, and strong, hooked beak; can swim but can't dive

VS.

ATLANTIC PUFFIN STATS

Length: 13 in (32 cm)
Wingspan: 21 in (53 cm)
Weight: 13 oz (369 g)
Top speed: 55 mph (89 kph) for short distance

Flies low and fast over water; expert swimmer and diver

HARRIS'S HAWK VS. JACKRABBIT: TEAMWORK

Most birds of prey hunt alone. But the Harris's hawks that live in the deserts of the southern United States are team players. They live in harsh environments, where prey is hard to find. So by hunting in groups of up to six, the hawks stand a better chance of getting a meal.

HUNTING TECHNIQUES

The birds stand on high perches and look around for the movement of a jackrabbit, a lizard, or a quail. Sometimes they stand on each other's backs to get a better view! If one bird sees movement, the others spread out to surround it, then fly at it from different directions so there's no escape. Then they share the kill. If the prey escapes this attack, the hawks fly after it until it is exhausted.

TEAMWORK: WORKING AS A GROUP TO ACHIEVE SOMETHING

JACKRABBIT

Jackrabbits have long ears and long hind legs. They can run very fast and may also "freeze" so their brown fur merges against the desert background – an effective camouflage. They may also run into thick desert vegetation or down burrows to escape a hunting hawk.

HARRIS'S HAWK STATS

Length: 18 - 23 in (46-59 cm)
Wingspan: up to 47 in (120 cm)
Weight: up to 30 oz (850 g)
Top speed: 50 mph (80 kph)

Intelligent; hunt in groups; excellent eyesight

VS.

JACKRABBIT STATS

Length: 24 in (61 cm)
Weight: 5 lbs (2.3 kg)
Top speed: 28 mph (45 kph)

Fast runner; alert; makes zig-zagging escape runs

CAMOUFLAGE: FUR OR SKIN MARKINGS THAT HELP AN ANIMAL HIDE IN ITS HABITAT

BIG FOOT

Harris's hawks have large and powerful feet and talons. They need to be strong to grip and lift large prey, such as a fully-grown jackrabbit!

LAMMERGEIER VS. TORTOISE: GRAVITY

Lammergeiers, or bearded vultures, have the strangest diet of any bird: they eat the marrow found inside bones. These gigantic birds of prey live in remote mountains in Asia, Africa, and Europe, where they soar high in the air in search of a meal. If one sees the skeleton of a sheep or goat, it swoops down, grabs a large bone and flies up to a height of up to 500 feet (152.4 m). When it is high enough, the bird drops the bone, which breaks open, revealing the protein-rich marrow inside.

DROPPED FROM ON HIGH

Lammergeiers sometimes do the same with live animals – tortoises, hyraxes, hares, and large lizards are plucked from the ground and dropped from a great height. The bird isn't interested in the soft flesh, just the animals' bones. The shell of a tortoise protects it from most predators, but it will break open if dropped from 165 feet (50.3 m)!

STRONG BODY AND WINGS ALLOW IT TO CARRY PREY OR LARGE BONES HIGH INTO THE AIR

POWERFUL STOMACH ACID DISSOLVES LARGE CHUNKS OF BONE

GRAVITY: THE FORCE THAT PULLS OBJECTS DOWN TO THE GROUND

HERMANN'S TORTOISE

The beautifully marked brown and yellow shell of a Hermann's tortoise protects it from above. It also has another shell called a plastron underneath its body. If it is threatened, the tortoise tucks its head and legs into its shell. Most of the time, this is enough to keep the tortoise safe, but if a lammergeier is particularly determined to eat it, then the tortoise will be taking an unexpected flight ...

MARROW: THE SOFT, FATTY SUBSTANCE INSIDE BONES

LAMMERGEIER STATS

Length: 4 ft (1.2 m)
Wingspan: 9 ft (2.7 m)
Weight: 15 lb (7 kg)
Top speed: 56 mph (90 kph)

Massive size; strong legs, talons and beak

VS.

TORTOISE STATS

Length: 11 in (28 cm)
Weight: 7 lb (3 .2 kg)
Top speed: less than 0.6 mph (1 kph)

Strong protective shell

ACID STOMACH

The bird swallows bits of bone as well as the marrow. This isn't a problem for a lammergeier, though: the strong acid in its stomach can dissolve any bone within a day.

SECRETARYBIRD VS. SPITTING COBRA: STAMPING

With its long legs, amazing crest of feathers, and graceful shape, a secretarybird doesn't look like a killer. These birds wander around the grasslands of Africa. Although secretarybirds are good fliers, they spend most of their time walking – up to 20 miles (32 km) in a day! From time to time they stamp one of their feet hard on the ground to disturb small animals – beetles, lizards, mice, and snakes.

STOMP, STOMP, STOMP!

When the bird finds prey, it raises one leg, then stomps down on its victim. It may kill a beetle or small lizard with one blow of its foot. For larger prey, such as mongooses or snakes, it may have to stamp several times. Then, the secretarybird swallows its meal whole.

STAMP: TO BRING A FOOT DOWN TO THE GROUND WITH FORCE

SPITTING COBRA

This snake kills frogs, lizards,and other snakes by biting them with its sharp fangs and injecting toxic venom. If threatened, the snake will spit venom into the face of its attacker. Having such long legs, a secretarybird's head is more than 3 feet (1 m) above the ground so it can usually avoid the deadly spit.

SECRETARYBIRD STATS

Length: 5 ft (1.5 m)
Wingspan: 7 ft (2.1 m)
Leg length: 2 ft (0.6 m)
Weight: 9 lb (4 kg)
Top speed: 2 mph (3 kph) when walking

Very long legs with stout toes, ideal for kicking; can deliver a powerful kick

VS.

SPITTING COBRA STATS

Length: 3 ft (1 m)
Weight: 6 oz (170 g)
Top speed: 6 mph (10 kph)

Attacks very quickly; spits venom

VENOM: TOXIC SUBSTANCE PRODUCED BY SOME ANIMALS

QUILL PENS

The birds are so named because the crest of feathers on the head reminded people of quill pens that secretaries used to write with in the 19th century.

GLOSSARY

adaptation features or skills that an animal species develops over time to thrive in its habitat

apex the very top; the top predator in a food chain with no natural enemies

bill a bird's beak

binocular vision eyesight where each of the two forward-facing eyes produces an image. These images overlap to give the animal an excellent ability to judge distance and depth

camouflage the patterns on an animal's fur, skin, or feathers that help it to hide in its habitat

carnivore an animal that eats only meat

dusk the time of day just before night when the Sun dips below the horizon

evolve to change over time

food chain a series of living things that depend on each other for food; each living thing is eaten by another living thing all the way up the food chain to the apex predator, which is not eaten by anything else

habitat the natural home of a plant or animal

herbivore an animal that eats only plants

hyrax a small herbivore mammal with a compact body and a short tail that lives in dry habitats in Africa and Asia; hyraxes look a bit like a large guinea pig, or a rabbit with short ears

ibex a type of wild mountain goat

ingenious clever; inventive

instinctive a behavior or an action that is done without having to think about it

invertebrate an animal without a backbone; spiders, insects, snails, and squid are all invertebrates

moorland open, wild land that is often covered with heather – a low-growing hardy plant; high moorlands are found on lower mountain slopes or in hilly areas

mammal a warm-blooded animal with a backbone and that has hair or fur at some stage in its life and is fed on its mother's milk when young

plumage a bird's feathers

predator an animal that hunts and kills other animals for food

prey/prey on an animal that is hunted for food (noun); to hunt and kill for food (verb)

reptile an animal with scaly skin, whose body temperature is the same as the environment around it. Reptiles may bask in the sun to warm up or seek shade to cool down

silhouette the dark shape or outline of a person or animal as seen against a bright background

territory an area of land defended by an animal against others of the same species

toxic something that is poisonous

FURTHER INFORMATION

BOOKS

Citizen Scientist: Studying Birds by Izzi Howell (Wayland, 2020)

Brutal Birds by Mignonne Gunasekara (Bearport, 2024)

The World's Greatest Predators by Mignonne Gunasekara (Jump!, Inc., 2024)

Wildlife Worlds (series) by Tim Harris (Franklin Watts, 2020)

WEBSITES

Check out the BBC bitesize website for lots of information relevant to this book and information on food chains.
www.bbc.co.uk/bitesize/topics/zx882hv/articles/z3c2xnb

National Geographic gives good introductions to the lifestyles of a range of birds. These are some of the best pages.

Barn owl: www.nationalgeographic.com/animals/birds/facts/barn-owl
Gannet: www.nationalgeographic.com/magazine/2012/08/gannets/
Golden eagle: www.nationalgeographic.com/animals/birds/g/golden-eagle/
Peregrine falcon: www.kids.nationalgeographic.com/animals/birds/peregrine-falcon/
Puffin: www.kids.nationalgeographic.com/animals/birds/atlantic-puffin/

This is a YouTube video of gannets diving.
www.youtube.com/watch?v=1Cp1n_vPvYY

INDEX